SUPER SPORTS

WATER SPORTS

DAVID JEFFERIS

Chrysalis Children's Books

First published in Great Britain in 2001 by
ⓢChrysalis Children's Books
An imprint of Chrysalis Books Group
The Chrysalis Building, Bramley Rd
London W10 6SP
Paperback edition first published in 2003
Copyright © David Jefferis/Alpha Communications 2001

A Belitha Book

Design and editorial production Alpha Communications
Educational advisor Julie Stapleton
Picture research Kay Rowley

ISBN 1 84138 346 5 (hb)
ISBN 1 84138 766 5 (pb)

British Library Cataloguing in Publication Data for this book is available from the British Library.
Acknowledgements
We wish to thank the following individuals and organizations for their help and assistance and for supplying material in their collections:
AllSport UK Ltd, Alpha Archive, Silvain Cazenave/Nikon, Club Med, Didier Givois, F. Monsis, Ker Robertson, Richard Martin, Stephen Munday, Matthieu Pendle, Loick Peyron, Philip Plisson, Ker Robertson, Pascal Rondeau, A. Sezerat, Sygma, Vandystadt Sports Photos, Nick Wilson, Yamaha, Y. Zedda

Diagrams by Gavin Page

Printed in China

10 9 8 7 6 5 4 3 2 1 (hb)
10 9 8 7 6 5 4 3 2 1 (pb)

▲ Hurtling down-river in a rubber raft can be an exciting ride! It's called white-water rafting, after the foam in the wildest parts of the river.

Contents

 Look out for the Super Sports Symbol

Look for the yacht silhouette in boxes like this.
Here you will find extra water sports facts, stories
and useful tips for beginners.

World of water sports

▲ Being a good swimmer helps if you're interested in water sports, but you don't have to be a sports champion.

▼ A ski-boat needs a big engine. Learning to water ski is not difficult, but you do have to balance well.

Power is needed for all water sports. Depending on the sport, this energy can come from the wind, a powerful engine, or your muscles!

The great thing about water sports is that you can have fun at almost any level. A trip to a swimming pool, canoeing and sailing can be just as exciting as an expensive power boat or an ocean-going yacht.

Safety is most important, so learn to swim well before trying the things in this book! Training is important too. A good teacher will show you the basics of a sport quickly and safely.

good water-skiers can use just one ski instead of a pair

▲ Wakeboarding uses a wide ski that can take off for a few seconds.

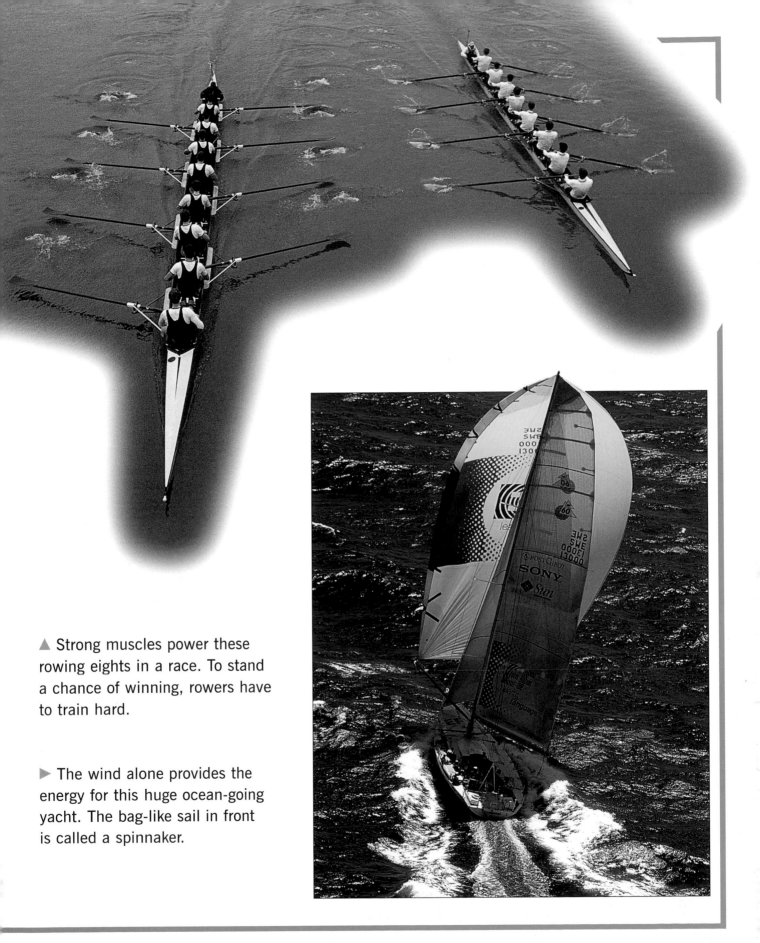

▲ Strong muscles power these rowing eights in a race. To stand a chance of winning, rowers have to train hard.

► The wind alone provides the energy for this huge ocean-going yacht. The bag-like sail in front is called a spinnaker.

Kayaks and canoes

Learning to use a kayak is a good introduction to water sports. But kayaking is trickier than it looks.

To a beginner, a kayak seems to have a mind of its own. It moves off easily, and for a few moments all seems fine. But then the kayak goes sideways – it just won't go in a straight line!

There is a trick to steering though, and once a kayaker learns to use the paddle correctly, a kayak become a very agile water craft.

▲ Kayaks are a type of canoe. They can be steered accurately through white water rapids.

▼ Safety is very important. Kayakers always wear a life jacket and a helmet. Life jackets are buoyant to help you float if you fall in the water.

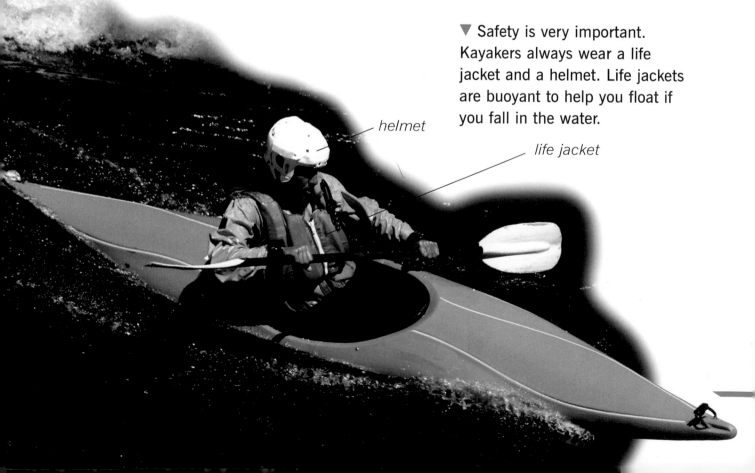

helmet

life jacket

▲ Canadian canoes are just right for exploring calmer waters, and are good fun for families.

Canadian canoes are modern versions of the birch-bark canoes first built by Native Americans to travel on rivers in North America.

Modern Canadian canoes are made of aluminium or plastic. These canoes can carry several people, and their supplies. For a family it's a great way to get everyone on the water.

 Look out – tight turn ahead!

Water sports are fun, but this true story shows that you should take care, even if you are in calm water.

A kayaker was exploring a stream, but when he tried to turn round, the boat caught both ends on the banks.

Moments later, the current flipped the boat over and the kayaker was head down in the water. Luckily, he got back up, helped by his life jacket.

White-water rafting

Rafting is great fun. Trained crews are in charge, but passengers have to paddle too.

▲ Over the edge! Rafters leave a mountain lake the quick way, straight down a waterfall.

White-water rafting is popular in mountain areas, where rivers rush with icy water from melting snow. Getting in a raft can be rather wobbly, as the rubber is soft and squashy. It is comfortable when you sit down, though. Everyone has a paddle, and when the raft captain gives out orders to paddle hard, the aim is keep clear of the sharp rocks on either side.

► These rafters show off one bad idea – no safety helmets. If you get thrown out, you can hit your head against a rock.

 Why use a raft made of rubber?

Rubber may seem to be a poor material for rafting – a sharp rock can cut a hole in it.

But rubber rafts are wide and stable, so it takes really rough water to tip one over.

A raft floats in a few centimetres of water, which allows it to skate over rocky shallows in safety. Lots of hand and foot straps help you cling on!

◀ It's all hands to the paddles to avoid the rocks either side of this fast-moving mountain stream.

supplies are packed in waterproof bags

Surfing the waves

strap fixes round wrist

Surfing is the sport of 'catching the wave'. Balancing on a board is not easy, and you have to guess when the best wave is coming.

You need a good sense of balance to surf well. Trying a short bougie-board is a good way to start, as you lie on your chest rather than standing up.

The next step is to go to a surf school and try the real thing. Expect to fall off the board a lot!

Once you have mastered the basic skills, you will want to be in the water for hours at a time.

▲ A bougie-board is cheap to buy, and easy to use. You lie on it, instead of standing up.

◄ A surfer needs skill to stay on the board through rough surf.

► The Pacific Ocean Hawaiian islands are famous for surfing – and with huge waves like this, you can see why!

◄ This eight-year-old French girl is an expert surfer.

⛵ Waiting for the perfect wave

Some of the highest tides in the world are along the coasts of Brittany, in France.

Keen surfers may start off at low tide, with waves no more than 50 cm high. On the right beach though, the incoming tide soon funnels the water into huge, foaming rollers, several metres high.

Then you swim out beyond the breakers, to wait for the 'big one', a wave that's big enough to ride all the way to shore.

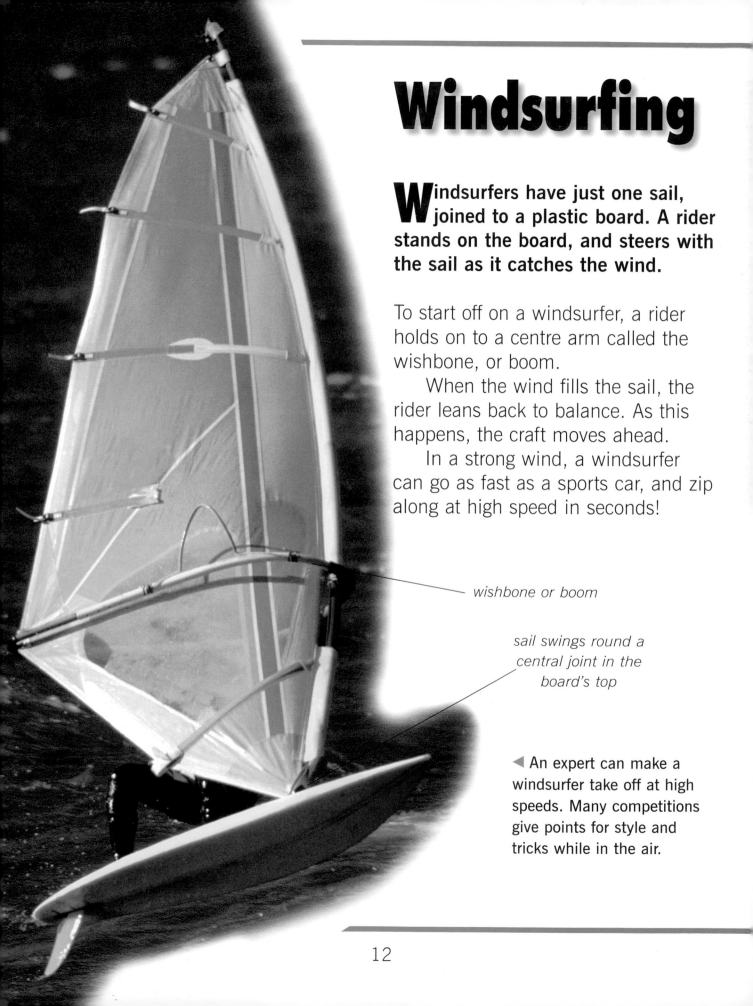

Windsurfing

Windsurfers have just one sail, joined to a plastic board. A rider stands on the board, and steers with the sail as it catches the wind.

To start off on a windsurfer, a rider holds on to a centre arm called the wishbone, or boom.

When the wind fills the sail, the rider leans back to balance. As this happens, the craft moves ahead.

In a strong wind, a windsurfer can go as fast as a sports car, and zip along at high speed in seconds!

wishbone or boom

sail swings round a central joint in the board's top

◀ An expert can make a windsurfer take off at high speeds. Many competitions give points for style and tricks while in the air.

▲ Experts can take off like this. But simply zooming along also gives lots of thrills.

▼ Windsurfer boards are made in many shapes and sizes. They all have footstraps and a slot for the sail.

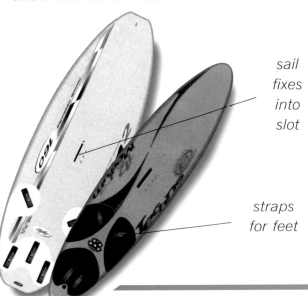

*sail
fixes
into
slot*

*straps
for feet*

 Brrr... don't get too cold!

To windsurf, you need to learn some sailing terms, be able to control the sail and steer the board in the water.

Learning the trick of getting your balance right takes some time, and you may spend much of your first day falling into the water. This doesn't hurt, but you mustn't let yourself get too cold.

The moment you start to shiver, it is time to come out of the water, have a hot drink and warm up.

Dinghy sailing

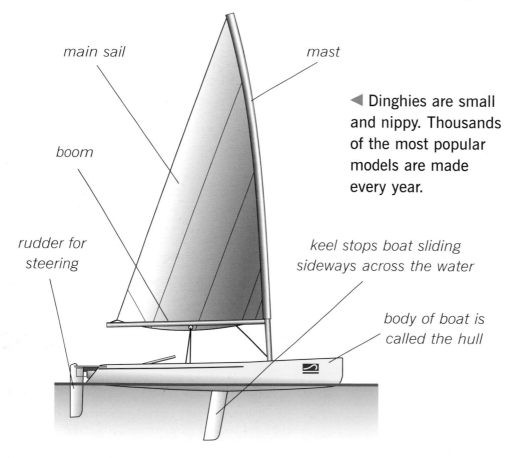

Dinghies are the smallest sail boats on the water. Most are designed for one or two crew and have a single sail.

Dinghies are easy to launch and have sails that are simple to rig up. Before long you can be good enough to compete in races. There are many types of dinghy. The most popular type is the Laser. Over 170 000 have been made.

▲ A dinghy sailor keeps the craft level by leaning out over the water.

main sail

mast

boom

rudder for steering

◄ Dinghies are small and nippy. Thousands of the most popular models are made every year.

keel stops boat sliding sideways across the water

body of boat is called the hull

► Letters on the sails of these Laser dinghies show countries that are racing – see if you can work out the ones in front!

▲ This Topaz dinghy has an open-ended hull to let water drain out. The hull is packed with foam and cannot sink.

⛵ Smoother is faster

Boat-builders are always trying to make their boats more efficient. One way is to make the hull of light and smooth plastics, instead of a traditional material like wood. A light boat can ride higher in the water, which gives less drag from waves. A smooth hull cuts through the water more easily.

You can feel the difference in these materials in your own home. Try stroking a plastic plate and a wooden chopping board. You will find the plastic much smoother.

race course is marked by these floating plastic buoys

Ocean racers

craft is 33.5m long

Huge ocean-going yachts are the queens of the seas. Many take part in long races, such as those across the Atlantic Ocean, or around the world.

▲ The Club Med is one of the fastest ocean-going yachts ever built.

The fastest ocean racers are multi-hull designs. Instead of just one hull, they have two (catamaran) or three (trimaran). Big multi-hulls are generally lighter than a traditional yacht of similar size, and can go faster.

These ocean racers are very big – the *Club Med* shown here has a mast more than 40m high. In early sea-tests, this 'big cat' covered a record 1007 km in one day of sailing – that's an average of 42 km/h!

▲ This yacht is named after a French travel company.

▲ Checking the sails on the tall mast is not a job for people scared of heights.

◄ Light but strong netting catches anyone who falls between the hulls.

Building an ocean giant

Designing and building a racing catamaran is a big job. It took 50 people nearly a year to build the twin hulls of this cat. The hulls are a sandwich of carbon-fibre, resin and fireproof materials. This mixture is light in weight, but strong enough to take the battering of ocean storms and gales.

The big cat needs a big crew during a race – 14 people are needed to sail the craft. It was built to compete in a round-the-world race, with a prize of $2 million.

crew wear helmets and life jackets

Power boats

Power boats are all about speed. They have a smooth, streamlined shape to cut through the water, and powerful engines for top speeds.

Power boats are the speed machines of the water. Even a small power boat can usually do at least 75 km/h. The most powerful boats can go much faster than this, at over 220 km/h.

If you like speed, then you will love power boats. But you have to be rich to own one. The price of the cheapest new boat is about £50 000. Bigger and faster ones can cost £500 000 or more!

▲ This is one of the fastest racing power boats, with room for four crew in the cockpit.

▶ These single-seat racers are called hydroplanes. They skate ('plane') on the water surface.

Like riding a boat on lumpy concrete

From a distance, a power boat looks as if it is gliding smoothly over the water.

Inside the cockpit, things are very different. When speeds go over 60 km/h, the ride turns very hard, and hitting a wave is like smashing into a lump of concrete.

When you ride in a power boat, you wear a helmet, life jacket, and strap yourself in very tightly. If you don't, you may get bruised or crack a rib.

Even so, while power boating is not a gentle sport, it is exciting and great fun.

▲ Some power boats have a catamaran design, with two hulls. Air is trapped between the hulls to give the boat a smoother ride.

Jet-ski boats

Jet-skis are like motorbikes on water. They are driven by a powerful jet of water, which squirts out of the back at high speed.

Riding a jet-ski is a real challenge. The machine bucks and bounces on the water, almost like a wild horse! It's easy to fall off, although a rider is unlikely to get hurt.

But jet-ski riders sometimes speed near beaches, and cause accidents with swimmers in the water. Good riders keep clear of beaches.

▲ You start off on your knees, kneeling on the jet-ski's rear platform. As speed builds up, you can get on to your feet.

speed is controlled by a small switch on the right hand-grip

centre bar moves up as the jet-ski gets up to speed

◄ You can lean into turns on a jet-ski, just like cornering on a motorbike. Pushing your weight to one side helps the jet-ski dig into the water for fast, tight turns.

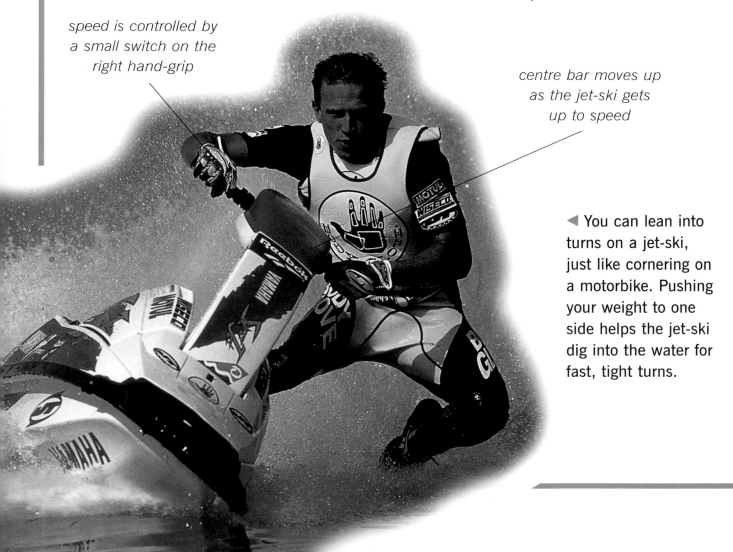

▲ Jet-ski racing is a high-speed sport, with riders
competing round a course laid out round floating markers.
Machines are fitted with specially-adjusted racing engines.

Scuba diving

Scuba equipment makes you free to explore under the sea. Start with a face mask and swim fins, then get trained for the real stuff.

You don't need to be super strong to go scuba diving, but you do need to be a good swimmer. Training usually begins with a short, 'taster' session. You try on the breathing kit, then use it during a dive in a safe pool. If you're keen, you can join a club and go for weekend courses. In a short time, you'll be ready for a real dive.

▲ Practise diving in a safe place, such as a swimming pool. Never dive alone. Scuba divers always have at least one dive-buddy in the water.

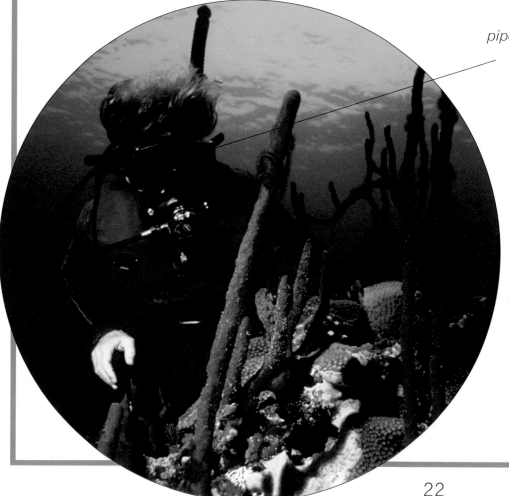

pipe takes air from tank to mouthpiece

◄ Once you are trained you can try exploring with other divers under the sea – perhaps finding an old wreck, or checking out amazing underwater plants.

► This is the dream of many scuba divers – reaching out to touch a friendly dolphin!

What is scuba gear?

The word scuba stands for 'self-contained underwater breathing apparatus'. It links an air tank with a special mouthpiece.

The mouthpiece is a clever bit of kit that gives you air exactly when you want it. You just breathe in through your mouth, and the correct amount of air flows.

Divers may also use a suit for warmth, weights for the right balance in the sea, and a pair of rubber swim fins, to move quickly.

New ideas

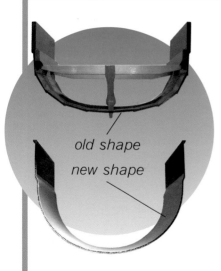

old shape
new shape

▲ Rowing boats now have U-shaped hulls. These are lighter and faster than traditional wood hulls (top).

Designers are constantly thinking up new ways to improve boats. And new water sports also appear from time to time.

Using new materials is one of the best ways to improve an old design. Few of today's boards and boats use heavy wood or metal. Instead, they are made mostly of lightweight mixtures of plastics and glues.

One new idea is combining different sports to make a new 'crossover' activity. An example is kitesurfing, in which a surfboard is towed behind a kite-like wing.

▲ Kitesurfing was developed during the 1990s. Kitesurfers surf and fly short distances.

flat, sail-like mast

▲ Oars have changed shape from long and thin to short and fat. The short style gives greater speed.

◀ Trimarans are among the fastest yachts. This one has a flattened mast that acts like a tall, thin sail, for extra speed.

hulls are joined by super-slim booms

Water sport facts

Here are some facts and stories from the world of water sports.

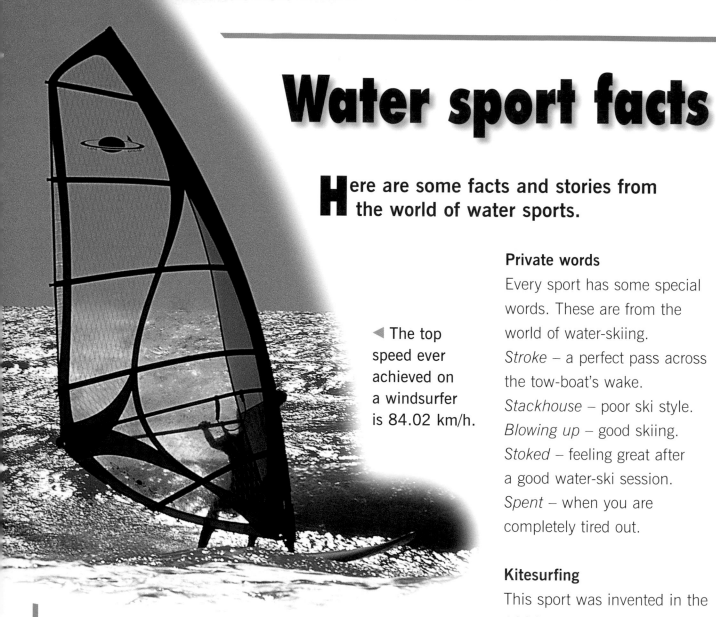

◄ The top speed ever achieved on a windsurfer is 84.02 km/h.

Private words

Every sport has some special words. These are from the world of water-skiing.

Stroke – a perfect pass across the tow-boat's wake.

Stackhouse – poor ski style.

Blowing up – good skiing.

Stoked – feeling great after a good water-ski session.

Spent – when you are completely tired out.

Kitesurfing

This sport was invented in the 1990s, and uses a large kite to pull a surfboard.

The added thrill is taking off for long airborne jumps, and doing stunts like spins, turns, even flying upside down for a few seconds.

Buggies can also be used for kiting from beaches. You sit in a small three-wheeler for high-speed thrills on, and above, the ground.

Chilly windsurfer

Dutchman Gerard-Jan Goekoop took the coldest windsurfing record in 1985, when he was ship's doctor on an Arctic research expedition.

When the ship was in pack ice near the North Pole, Goekoop put on a wet suit, then went windsurfing in the icy waters by the ship!

Long jumpers

Top water-skiers aim to make record-breaking jumps off shallow ramps, which are set up to float in mid-water.

The best water-skiers can fly long distances through the air after zooming off a ramp at speed. The women's world record water-ski jump is 52.4m, the men's is 68.2m.

Secret signals

Scuba divers need a way to signal underwater. They can't talk, so a hand-signal system does the job.

Scuba signs include:

Thumb up – Going up.

Thumb down – Going down.

Arm up – stop where you are.

Fist shaken from side to side – distress or emergency.

▲ A scuba diver heads toward the sea bottom.

High speed kayaks

In 1995 four Hungarians paddled at 23.11 km/h over a 200m course. A year later, a German team covered a longer 1000m course only slightly slower, at 20.98 km/h.

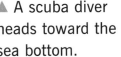

◄ Big yachts are long-haul champions of the seas. Smaller craft are faster over short distances. The record is 86.21 km/h over 500m, by a two-man trimaran.

Surfing money-maker

US surfer Kelly Slater has earned the most money from his sport – when he retired in 1998, he had made £427 313, much of it from surf-gear makers who pay him to wear their products.

Record rowing

The fastest rowing speed by one person is 16.47 km/h, achieved in 1994, by Canadian rower Silken Laumann. Team boats are faster still – an eight-man Dutch team hit 22.22 km/h over 2000m in 1996.

▲ A family-size power boat can also tow skiers.

Water sport words

Here are some technical terms used in this book.

bougie board
A board that is suitable for beginners – instead of standing up, you simply lie on your chest. Also known as a body board.

buoy
A floating marker that shows such things as a race-course or position of rocks. Buoys are anchored by chain to the sea bottom, so they stay in place, even in strong wind or tides.

dinghy
A small, open sailing boat. Dinghies usually have just one or two sails. Early types were made of wood. Modern ones are usually made of plastics.

dive buddy
One of a two-person diving team. Sport divers always go in pairs, so there is someone to help in case of emergency.

hull
The main body of a boat or ship. Small craft may have hulls of wood or plastics. Large ships have metal hulls.

hydroplane
A speed boat made to skate across the water surface. Craft made with a deeper, v-shape hull cut through the water.

kayak
A type of canoe, now made of plastics. The first kayaks were made by the Inuit people of North America, who used a covering of seal skin.

keel
The bottom spine of a boat or ship. On windsurfers, the keel is known as a daggerboard, and is moveable.

kitesurfing
A sport in which your feet are fixed to a board, similar to a snowboard. Power comes from a large kite-like wing, which tows you through the water. On windy days, high jumps and aerial stunts are possible.

life jacket
Clothing that keeps you afloat if you fall in water. The best jackets keep you face-up, so your mouth and nose are above water level.

◄ This water-skier wears a life jacket in case of a bad fall.

multi-hull

A seacraft with more than one hull. A catamaran has a pair of hulls, joined by booms. A trimaran has a centre hull with outriggers on either side.

power boat

A vessel built to zoom along at high speed. Power boats range from single-seaters with outboard motors to massive craft capable of 200 km/h.

rowing eight

A rowing boat designed for an eight-person crew. There is usually a cox as well, who steers the boat. Other rowing boats include designs for four, two and one person.

sandwich construction

A method of making a boat hull. It is made by building up layers of stiff carbon-fibre, mixed with resin and glue. Other fireproof materials are often included. The result is a material much lighter and stronger than wood or metal.

scuba

Self-contained underwater breathing apparatus. An air tank is linked to a mouthpiece by a rubber pipe. Scuba gear was invented by the French explorer Jacques Cousteau, with Emil Gagnon, in 1943.

spinnaker

Bag-like sail used on sailing boats. Spinnakers are good for speed in light winds, and when sailing down-wind.

wakeboard

Wide board towed behind a ski-boat. On a wakeboard, you make jumps off the spray (or wake) behind the boat. You can also do rolls and stunts.

white water

Name for the foaming waters in fast-flowing river sections.

wishbone

Oval-shaped handle used to control a windsurfer sail. Also known as a boom.

◄ A wakeboard, packed ready for use.

◄ A ski-boat trails a foaming wake.

Water science

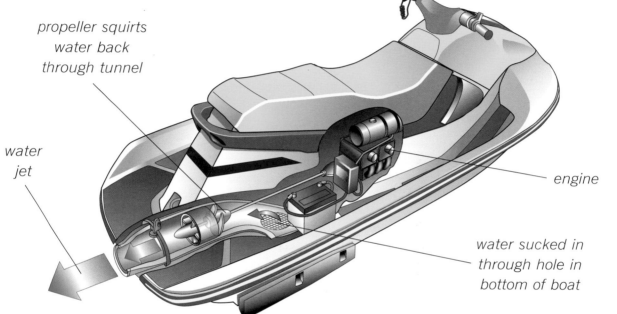

There is plenty to learn about the how-and-why of water sports and sporting machines.

▲ Jet-skis are also known as PWCs, or personal water craft.

propeller squirts water back through tunnel

water jet

engine

water sucked in through hole in bottom of boat

Rocket on water

A jet-ski uses the principle of action and reaction to move. Water squirts out of the back (the action), so the jet-ski moves forward (the reaction). Try this project to see how it works.

1 Fill an empty plastic drink bottle with cold water.

2 Push a cork into the top. Fix it firmly but not tightly.

3 Lay the bottle in a bath. Push hard, and the cork will whiz out!

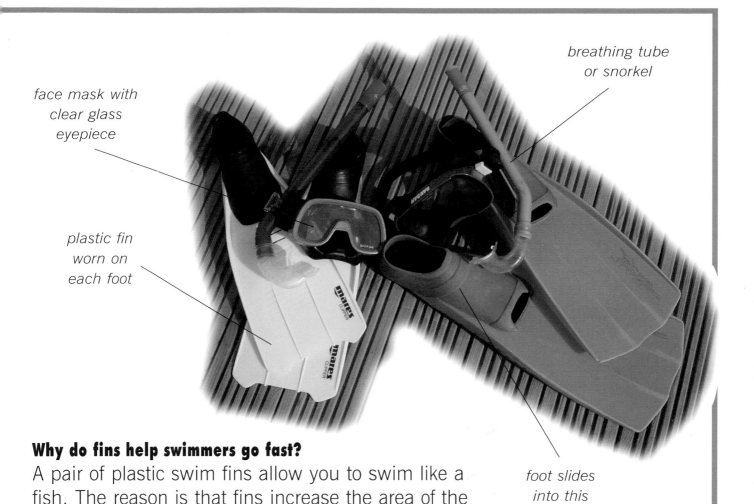

face mask with
clear glass
eyepiece

plastic fin
worn on
each foot

breathing tube
or snorkel

foot slides
into this
part

Why do fins help swimmers go fast?

A pair of plastic swim fins allow you to swim like a fish. The reason is that fins increase the area of the feet, so giving a swimmer more pushing power.

1 You need a small and a large paddle. We used a kitchen spatula and board.

2 Fill a bath with cold water, and paddle hard with the spatula to make waves.

3 Now use the board. You will see that its extra size shifts much more water.

Index